THE GREAT AUSTRALIAN PUMPKIN RECIPE BOOK

© Copyright 1992 by
Southern Holdings Pty Ltd
ACN 009550841
This edition published 2005

ISBN 094 9089 16 8

Text by Barbara Carr
Illustrations by Nola Hammond and David Hammond

The cover picture...

Robert Allen, 2, proudly shows off the two huge pumpkins which won first and second in this year's contest at the Huonville Bowls Club. The monster on the left was grown by Robert's grandfather, Colin Voss, and weighed in at an incredible 92.5kg,or 204lb. The other large pumpkin was grown by Robert's uncle, Dean Voss.

The picture first appeared in the SOUTHERN STAR, with the following story...

Colin's Secret Lies in the Pumpkin Patch

Huonville Bowls Club member Colin Voss is not a secretive man - he always has been known to answer *almost* any question that comes his way.

Almost because when the subject turns to pumpkins, he becomes very evasive.

Mystery has surrounded Colin's success over the past five years in winning the prize for the heaviest pumpkin grown for the club's annual pumpkin-growing contest.

This year he did it again, producing a monstrous specimen weighing in at 92.5kg (240lb). And as much as they tried, none of his other mates at the bowls club could top the weight.

This year's pumpkin is the largest Colin has ever grown - the next largest was a paltry 78kg (172lb) vegetable four years ago.

Closest to Colin this year was his son, Dean, who in his first year managed an 83.9kg (185lb) entry.

All Colin would say about his success was that the pumpkins needed lots of fertiliser.

Colin said the competition was pretty serious, although the competition was just for a bit of fun.

"There is a $2 entry fee for everyone who enters and the winner takes all. It is just enough to buy your cobbers a beer and that's about it," he said.

Colin is a nurseryman and market gardener, so it is logical that he should do well in the competition. But to win every year can be a little frustrating for the other competitors.

This frustration has led to some light-hearted foul play over the years with pumpkins being hollowed out and filled with all sorts of things.

The president of the Huonville Bowls Club, Mr Stan Bell, said that the competitors were amazed at Colin winning the event and were looking for more entries to increase the competition.

"One year we had one guy who hollowed one out and filled it up with nails, but now there is usually a metal detector on hand and a chainsaw to check the authenticity of the entrants," Mr Bell said.

Whatever Colin's special formula, all anyone can be sure of is that next year he will be the one to beat.

* *

Contents

We may live without poetry,
          music and art;
We may live without conscience,
          and live without heart;
We may live without friends;
          we may live without books;
But civilized man cannot live
          without cooks.

He may live without books,
          - what is knowledge but grieving?
He may live without hope,
          - what is hope but deceiving?
He may live without love,
          - what is passion but pining?
But where is the man who can
          live without dining?

Owen Meredith

'When at table, Johnson was totally absorbed in the business of the
moment; his looks seemed rivetted to his plate; nor would he,
unless when in very high company, say one word, or even pay the
least attention to what was said by others, till he had satisfied his
appetite, which was so fierce and indulged with such intenseness
that while in the act of eating, the veins of his forehead swelled and
generally a strong perspiration was evident. To those whose
sensations were delicate, this could not but be disgusting; and it
was doubtless not very suitable to the character of a philosopher,
who should be distinguished by self-command.'

Boswell

'Let me smile with the wise, and feed with the rich.'

Johnson

PUMPKIN AND BREAD SOUP

1/4 cup vegetable or olive oil
1 - 2 cloves garlic, peeled (or to taste)
1kg pumpkin, peeled, seeded and diced
3-1/2 cups chicken stock (or water)
1/2 teaspoon salt
2 slices stale bread (white), remove crusts and dice
1 teaspoon dried basil
2 tablespoons finely chopped parsley
1/4 teaspoon black pepper

Heat oil and garlic cloves in large saucepan for a few minutes. Do not allow garlic to burn. Remove garlic. Add diced pumpkin & salt, and cook until pumpkin is slightly softened. Add stock/water, cover and simmer 25 minutes until pumpkin is soft, stirring occasionally. Add bread, basil & pepper, simmer on low heat 2 - 3 minutes.

Put soup through blender and return to saucepan to reheat. Serve sprinkled with parsley.

CURRIED PUMPKIN SOUP

2 tablespoons light olive oil   1 large onion
750g chopped peeled pumpkin   2 teaspoons curry powder
250g chopped peeled potato   pepper
about 2 tablespoons chicken stock powder

Saute chopped vegetables in olive oil over medium heat till becoming slightly soft. Add chicken stock powder and curry powder, cover and saute over low heat for one minute.

Add enough water to not quite cover the vegetables. Bring to the boil, reduce heat and simmer till vegetables are soft. Push through a sieve or blend in a blender. Return to saucepan, add pepper, and gently bring to boil. Serves 4.

PUMPKIN AND BEAN SOUP

180g cooked dried blackeyed peas
2 teaspoons dried onion flakes or 30g diced onion.
60g diced pumpkin
30g finely diced celery
360ml chicken stock made with one stock cube

Combine all ingredients in saucepan. Simmer 40 minutes or until vegetables are tender and soup is thick.

Serves 1.

ORIENTAL PUMPKIN SOUP

1 medium sized pumpkin (1-1/2 kg)
1-1/2 litres chicken stock
100g butter   1 teaspoon coriander
milk of one coconut   salt, pepper

Peel the pumpkin, remove seeds and cut into slices. Boil in the chicken stock and butter, adding coriander, salt and pepper. When the pumpkin is cooked (about 30 minutes) put the lot in a blender or push through a sieve. Return to the saucepan and add the coconut milk. Reheat but do not boil.

If possible, garnish with fresh basil. May be eaten hot or cold.

PUMPKIN SOUP

500g pumpkin   3-1/2 cups chicken stock
1 carrot   1/4 teaspoon nutmeg
2 onions   salt, pepper

Peel pumpkin, carrot and onions; cut into pieces. Put all vegetables in pan. Add chicken stock and nutmeg, salt and pepper. Bring to boil; reduce heat, simmer covered until pumpkin is tender. Puree in blender or food processor or push through sieve. Chill. Serve with spoonful of sour cream and chopped chives. Serves 4.

PUMPKIN SOUP WITH YOGHURT

1 tablespoon sunflower oil	450g pumpkin
225g tomatoes	225g carrots
2 teaspoons dried basil	850mls water
freshly ground black pepper	1 onion
150mls natural yoghurt	25g unsalted butter

Peel, de-seed and chop pumpkin. Wash, trim and slice carrots. Place the vegetables in a large pan with the water. Bring to the boil. Simmer for 20 minutes until the vegetables are tender. Drain and reserve the cooking water.

Peel and finely chop the onion. Saute in butter and oil until soft. Chop the tomatoes coarsely and mix with the onions. Cook a further 5 minutes. Put the pumpkin, onion and tomato mixture and 275mls of cooking water into a liquidizer or push through a sieve. Return to the pan. Season to taste with basil and black pepper. Heat thoroughly. Pour into serving bowls and swirl a little yoghurt in each before serving.

3

CREAM OF PUMPKIN SOUP

2 small onions, chopped
25g butter
1.3kg pumpkin, cooked and sieved
little grated cheese
chopped parsley (optional)

600ml water
salt and pepper
2 eggs, beaten
600mls milk

Fry the onions lightly in the butter and put into a pan with the sieved pumpkin, water and seasonings; simmer for about 2 hours. Mix the eggs with the milk, add to the soup, and heat very gently for a further few minutes to cook the egg, taking care to prevent curdling. Add the cheese and the parsley (if used) just before serving. (serves 6)

CHILLED PUMPKIN SOUP

1-1/2kg Queensland blue or butternut pumpkin
2 tablespoons butter
1 clove garlic, crushed
12 spring onions, finely chopped
3 cups light chicken stock

salt and pepper
2 cups milk
croutons
1 spring onion, finely sliced

Peel and roughly chop the pumpkin. Heat the butter and saute garlic and spring onions until a light golden colour. Add the pumpkin and stock and simmer, covered, for 20 minutes or until the pumpkin is tender.

Remove from the heat and allow to cool, then puree the pumpkin mixture in a blender or push through a sieve.

Season to taste with salt and pepper, add the milk and mix well. Chill. Serve garnished with crisp fried croutons and fine slices of spring onions. Serves 8.

PUMPKIN & VEGETABLE SOUP WITH HERBED DAMPER

1 tablespoon chopped fresh parsley
4 cups water
2 small chicken stock cubes, crumbled
1 cup lentil sprouts

300g pumpkin, chopped	***Herbed damper***
1 onion, chopped	1-1/3 cups self-raising flour
2 potatoes, chopped	2/3 cup wholemeal self-raising flour
2 carrots, chopped	15g polyunsaturated margarine
2 zucchini, chopped	2 tablespoons chopped fresh parsley
410g can tomatoes	2 teaspoons chopped fresh thyme
1 clove garlic, crushed	1 cup milk, approximately

Combine pumpkin, onion, potatoes, carrots, zucchini, undrained tomatoes, garlic, parsley, water and stock cubes in a large saucepan, bring to the boil over high heat, then reduce heat and simmer, covered, for about 20 minutes. Alternatively, microwave on high for about 15 minutes, or until all of the vegetables are cooked.

Stir in the lentil sprouts, cook over medium heat for a further 2 minutes, or microwave on high for about 2 minutes. Serve with herb scones.

Herbed damper

Sift flours into a medium bowl, rub in margarine. Stir in parsley, thyme and enough milk to mix to a soft dough. Turn dough onto a lightly floured surface, knead lightly until smooth, press out to give a 2 cm thickness. Cut into wedges or cut out as scones. Place scones into a lightly greased 20cm sandwich pan, brush tops with remaining milk. Bake in a very hot oven for about 15 minutes, or until tops are browned and scones sound hollow when tapped. Serves 4.

5

PUMPKIN & VEGETABLE SOUP

1.2 litres stock   45g butter
chopped parsley   2 tablespoons flour
2 cups pumpkin, carrots, celery, onion and potatoes.

Melt butter and fry the vegetables lightly. Sprinkle with flour and cook for 5 minutes.

Add stock and allow to simmer gently for 15-20 minutes. Just before serving, sprinkle with chopped parsley. Serves 4-6.

PUMPKIN & LEEK SOUP

500g pumpkin, peeled and diced   225ml reduced cream
250g potatoes, peeled and diced   3 leeks sliced
2 chicken soup stock tablets   45g butter
cayenne pepper to taste   4 cups water
2 tablespoons chopped parsley

In a saucepan saute pumpkin, potatoes and leeks in melted butter until slightly soft. Add water and stir in chicken soup stock tablets. Cover and simmer 20 minutes or until vegetables are tender. Puree in a food processor or blender or push through a sieve. Return to saucepan, reheat and stir in cayenne pepper and reduced cream. Do not boil. Serve sprinkled with chopped parsley. Serves 4.

PUMPKIN SOUP SERVED IN THE SHELL

1 small pumpkin   1 teaspoon nutmeg
125g butter   4 litres meat stock
2-3 cups finely chopped onion   salt and pepper to taste
2-3 cloves crushed garlic   1 cup cream
1 orange or lemon cut into quarters   4 sprigs parsley
parsley or chives to garnish

Wash pumpkin. Cut off a lid at stalk end. Leave in place and bake in a moderate oven until flesh is tender. Test with a fork after two hours. Take from oven and leave to cool.

Remove lid, carefully scoop out seeds and then the flesh.

In a large saucepan melt butter, add onions and garlic, cook until soft. Add all remaining ingredients except cream and simmer for 20 minutes. Take out citrus pieces and put soup through a sieve or a blender. Return to saucepan and just before serving gently stir in cream and sprinkle chopped chives or parsley on top.

Heat the pumpkin shell serving bowl in a warm oven for 15 minutes before filling with the soup. Bring to the table complete with lid.

GOLDEN SOUP

3 teaspoons margarine
1 medium onion peeled & chopped
1 clove garlic, crushed (optional)
1 stalk celery, chopped
750g pumpkin, peeled & cubed
4 cups chicken stock (or use bouillon cubes)
2 teaspoons finely chopped fresh marjoram OR 1/2 teaspoon dried
1 bay leaf   1 cup buttermilk
1/4 teaspoon pepper   parsley

In a large, heavy based saucepan melt margarine over moderate heat. Add onion, garlic, celery. Cook about 5 minutes or until the onion is soft.

Add remaining ingredients except buttermilk and parsley. Bring to boil, reduce heat until just simmering, cover and cook until pumpkin is tender, about 20 minutes. Remove from heat. Discard bay leaf. Cool 5 minutes.

puree soup in a blender or food processor. Return to saucepan and stir in buttermilk. Reheat gently but do not boil. Ladle into bowls and garnish with parsley. Serves 6.

PUMPKIN AND POTATO SOUP

750g pumpkin
2 large onions or leeks
250g potatoes
3 chicken stock cubes

1 litre water
1 cup cream
salt and pepper to taste

Peel pumpkin, cut into small pieces, put into a large saucepan. Add peeled and chopped onions or sliced leeks, peeled and chopped potatoes, crumbled stock cubes and water. Bring to boil, reduce heat and simmer uncovered 25 minutes or until vegetables are very soft and tender. Push vegetables and liquid through fine sieve or puree in blender. Return puree to saucepan, add cream, salt and pepper. Bring to boil, stirring. Reduce heat, simmer further five minutes then serve.

MICROWAVE PUMPKIN AND CORN SOUP

2 onions, chopped
1 tablespoon chopped chives
1 butternut pumpkin, peeled and diced
60g butter
3-1/2 cups chicken stock
440g can creamed corn
3 teaspoons worcestershire sauce
1/2 cup cream

Combine pumpkin, onions and butter in a large bowl, cover, cook on High for 3 minutes. Add chicken stock and cover, cook on High for 25 minutes. Puree in a blender or processor, stir in corn, worcestershire sauce and add cream, reheat, sprinkle with chives. Serves 6.

SPICED PUMPKIN SOUP

1 large onion, chopped
1 medium potato, peeled and diced
salt and freshly-ground pepper
4 cups chicken stock or water
cream to finish

1 kg pumpkin
60g butter
10 coriander seeds
1/2 teaspoon cumin

Peel and roughly dice the pumpkin. Put into a pan with the butter, onion, spices and potato. Cover with a lid and simmer over a gentle heat for about 15 minutes, until very tender.

Blend the soup in a blender or food processor or push through a sieve. Reheat gently, check for seasoning and serve with a spoonful of cream floating in each bowl. Scatter a little parsley over if desired.

PUMPKIN AND BACON

500g pumpkin, peeled and chopped
2 bacon rashers cut in 2cm strips
1 medium onion, peeled and chopped
30g soft butter or margarine
1 cup fresh breadcrumbs

1/3 cup water
1/2 teaspoon salt
1 egg, beaten
2 teaspoons sugar

Cook bacon in medium frying pan about 5 minutes or until crisp. Place bacon on paper towel until needed. Heat oven 180C then add pumpkin and onion to dripping in frying pan. Cook for 2 minutes, add water, cover and cook about 15 minutes or until vegetables are tender.

Mash pumpkin and onion with a potato masher. Add butter, salt, sugar, egg and breadcrumbs. Mix thoroughly. Pour into buttered casserole dish and sprinkle with crumbled bacon strips. Bake uncovered for 20 minutes.

QUICK SAUTEED PUMPKIN

1 medium butternut pumpkin
60g butter or margarine
2 tablespoons finely chopped parsley
1/2 teaspoon salt
1/4 teaspoon ground nutmeg
1/4 teaspoon black pepper

Cut pumpkin in 6mm slices; peel, remove seeds and fibre. Melt butter in large frying pan, add pumpkin slices and salt. Cover and cook on moderate heat 20 minutes or until tender, turning slices frequently. Season before serving.

SPICY BAKED PUMPKIN

1 large butternut pumpkin   pinch ground nutmeg
60g butter or margarine   pinch ground allspice
1 tablespoon brown sugar

Heat oven 200C and melt butter in medium casserole dish in oven. Peel pumpkin, remove seeds and cut into chunks. Add pumpkin chunks to casserole dish, coating them with butter. Bake (uncovered) 15 minutes, then coat again with butter. Bake 10 minutes, then sprinkle with mixed sugar and spices. Bake 5 minutes and serve with a little butter over each piece.

BOILED PUMPKIN IN WINE

2 tablespoons soy sauce
2-1/2 cups soup stock or water
700g pumpkin, peeled, seeds removed, cut into 2.5cm cubes

2 tablespoons white wine
2 tablespoons sugar

Bring wine, sugar, soy sauce and stock or water to boil. Add pumpkin, return to boil, cover, reduce heat and simmer until tender, 10-15 minutes. Drain and serve hot with or without cooking liquid.

WHOLEMEAL PUMPKIN AND CHIVE QUICHE

Pastry
1 cup wholemeal plain flour
1/4 cup wholemeal self-raising flour
1/4 cup wheatgerm or unprocessed bran
125g butter
2 tablespoons water, approximately
Filling

15g butter
1 small onion, finely chopped
3 bacon rashers, finely chopped
1 cup cooked, mashed pumpkin

3 eggs
300ml carton cream
1/2 cup grated tasty cheese
1 tablespoon chopped chives

Sift flours into bowl, add wheatgerm. Rub in butter, add enough water to mix to a firm dough, cover, refrigerate 30 minutes. Roll pastry out large enough to line a 23cm flan tin, trim edges, line with greaseproof paper, fill with dry beans or rice. Bake in moderately hot oven 7 minutes, remove paper and beans, bake further 7 minutes.

Melt butter in pan, add onion and bacon, cook, stirring, until onion is soft; combine pumpkin, eggs, cream, cheese and chives in bowl, whisk in onion mixture.

Pour filling into pastry case, bake in moderate oven for about 30 minutes or until set.

CHEESE & PUMPKIN

250g cooked, mashed pumpkin	pepper and salt to taste
250g grated cheese	1 tablespoon margarine
1/2 cup boiling milk	2 eggs
2 tablespoons sifted S.R. flour	4 thick slices of bread

Melt all the cheese (except 1 heaped tablespoon) in the boiling milk over low heat. Put pumpkin, pepper and salt, melted cheese and milk, sifted flour and 2 eggs into a bowl and beat well until smooth. Pour into a greased pie dish or casserole. Crumble bread and sprinkle evenly on top. Dot with margarine

Bake in hot oven for 30 minutes. Take out and sprinkle remaining cheese. Bake until set.

For a change, cut and chip pumpkin the same as potato chips. Deep fry with potato chips. A mixture of pumpkin and potato chips adds colour to a plate.

POTATO PUMPKIN CAKES

1 potato sized piece peeled pumpkin
1 large potato   1 egg
1 small onion   1 tablespoon oil
1 clove garlic, crushed   1 tablespoon light soy sauce
pinch of pepper   1 tablespoon chopped parsley

Peel potato and grate. Place in colander, rinse in cold water, squeeze out liquid by pressing with wooden spoon.

Grate pumpkin, grate peeled onion. Mix all vegetables with garlic, soy sauce, pepper and parsley. Shape into 4 patties.

Heat oil in frying pan and cook patties about 2 minutes, or until set and golden. Turn and brown other side. Reduce heat and cook 3 - 4 minutes, turning once. Serve hot as a vegetable or as a light lunch with salad.

HAM, PUMPKIN AND APPLE

500g fully cooked ham slice
250g cooked pumpkin, in small chunks, drained
2 apples, sliced thin
2 tablespoons brown sugar
2 tablespoons orange juice
1 tablespoon butter or margarine

In a skillet, brown ham slice on one side; turn. Arrange pumpkin and apple around ham. Sprinkle with brown sugar and orange juice, dot with butter. Cover and cook 5 minutes or until apples are tender and ham and pumpkin are heated, basting several times with pan juices. Serves 4.

STUFFED PUMPKIN

1x1 kg pumpkin (cut slice off stem end and hollow out seeds and fibre)
1/3 cup green peas or 1/3 cup French beans, parboiled
1 cup cooked chicken or pork, diced
1/2 cup shrimps, cooked

3 tablespoons white wine	salt
1 tablespoon soy sauce	2 tablespoons oil
1 tablespoon sugar	1 medium onion, thinly sliced
1 tablespoon cornflour	1 medium carrot, grated
3 eggs, beaten	1/3 cup mushrooms, sliced

Pre-heat oven to 350F (175C). Lightly salt inside of pumpkin. Heat oil in a heavy pan, add onions and saute until lightly browned. Add carrots and then mushrooms, sauteeing each lightly as added. Combine sauteed vegetables and remaining ingredients and stuff pumpkin with mixture. Place sliced stem back on top, brush oil on the outer skin and place on a greased baking tin. Bake for 30-40 minutes or until tender.

Alternatively, pumpkin can be steamed in a covered steamer for 30-40 minutes or until tender.

PUMPKIN WITH FRANKFURTERS

360g pumpkin	2 teaspoons margerine
180g cocktail frankfurters	pinch cinnamon
1/2 teaspoon maple syrup	

Wash and cut pumpkin in half. Remove seeds. Bake pumpkin cut side down on foil-lined shallow baking tin at 375F (190C), for 40 minutes. Remove from oven. Stir 1/4 teaspoon maple syrup into each half. Place 4 oz (120g) cocktail frankfurters in each pumpkin half. Return to baking tin. Reduce oven to 350F (180C) and bake 30 minutes. Dot each half with one teaspoon margarine and pinch of cinnamon and return to oven for a minute. Serves 2.

HOT AND SPICY STUFFED GOLDEN NUGGET

6 golden nugget pumpkins
1/4 cup oil
Filling

500g lean minced beef	2 teaspoons ground cumin
2 teaspoons oil	1/2 teaspoon chilli powder
15g butter	2 bacon rashers
400g can tomatoes	1/2 cup dry white wine
1 onion, chopped	2 tablespoons tomato paste
432g can red kidney beans, drained	1 clove garlic, crushed

Cut a 3cm lid from each pumpkin, scoop out seeds. Brush inside and out of each pumpkin with oil, place pumpkins on oven tray, place oiled lids on top; bake in moderate oven 30 minutes.

Heat butter and oil in large pan, add onion, bacon, chilli and cumin, stir over heat few minutes or until onion is soft, pour into bowl. Add beef to pan, cook, stirring, until well browned; add onion mixture, garlic, tomato paste, wine, undrained crushed tomatoes and beans. Cook over low heat, stirring occasionally, for about 20 minutes or until mixture is thick.

Place filling into pumpkins, top with lid, return to tray, bake in moderate oven 30 minutes or until pumpkins are tender. Serves 6.

FRIED PUMPKIN BLOSSOMS

1/2 cup milk	pumpkin blossoms
1/2 cup flour	oil for deep frying
1 egg	

Make a thin batter using egg, milk, and flour. Dip the pumpkin blossoms in the batter and fry in hot oil. Serve as you would any vegetable.

STUFFED GOLDEN NUGGET

4 golden nugget pumpkins
1 tablespoon oil
Filling

1 tomato, peeled and chopped
3/4 cup brown rice
2-1/2 cups water
1 large vegetable stock cube, crumbled
125g mushrooms, finely chopped
1 tablespoon chopped fresh basil

1 tablespoon oil
2 cloves garlic, crushed
1 onion, chopped

Cut a slice from top of each pumpkin, reserve tops, remove and discard seeds. Cut a slice from base of pumpkins so pumpkins will stand securely. Press filling firmly into pumpkins, place on an oven tray, replace tops, brush with oil. Bake in moderate oven for about 45 minutes, or until pumpkins are tender. Cut into wedges to serve.

Filling

Heat oil in a large frying pan, add garlic, onion and tomato, stir over high heat for about 2 minutes, or until onion is soft. Stir in rice and combined water and stock cube, bring to the boil, then reduce heat, cover and simmer for about 30 minutes, or until all liquid is absorbed. Remove pan from heat, stir in mushrooms and basil. Serves 8.

PUMPKIN AND BACON DAMPER

375g chopped pumpkin
1 tablespoon milk
1 egg, lightly beaten
1 onion, chopped
2 bacon rashers, chopped

1 teaspoon dry mustard
1/4 teaspoon cayenne pepper
2-1/2 cups self-raising flour
60g butter

Boil, steam or microwave pumpkin until tender. Drain, push through a sieve. Stir in milk and egg. Cook onion and bacon in pan until lightly browned, remove from heat. Sift mustard, pepper and flour into bowl, rub in butter, add bacon and onion. Stir in pumpkin mixture. Turn onto lightly floured surface, knead lightly until smooth.

Press out to 3cm thickness with hand, place dough into large, greased, heavy-based shallow pan or place directly onto greased barbecue plate. Using a sharp knife, mark into wedges 1cm deep. Place pan on barbecue plate, cook over medium heat until damper is cooked through; this will take about 30 minutes. Turn damper several times during the cooking. Serve hot with butter.

PUMPKIN VEGETABLE AND CHEESE HARLEQUIN

500g Pumpkin, broccoli, french beans, squash and zucchini
60g butter, melted

125g tasty cheese, cubed or crumbled
2 tablespoons mixed chopped herbs e.g. parsley, chives, oregano, thyme.
2 tablespoons pine nuts

Steam or microwave a selection of vegetables until just tender. Add the melted butter, herbs and cheese and toss lightly.

Serve immediately garnished with toasted pine nuts. Serves 4.

PUMPKIN AND VEGETABLE LASAGNE

1/2 cup plain flour
1/4 cup oat bran
3 eggs, lightly beaten
1 cup milk
1/2 cup freshly grated
  parmesan cheese

Sauce
30g butter
1 tablespoon plain flour
1 tablespoon oat bran
1-1/4 cups milk

Filling
15g butter
1 clove garlic, crushed
1 onion, finely chopped
2 sticks celery, chopped
3 medium zucchini, sliced
500g pumpkin, chopped
425g can tomatoes
2x440g cans baked beans

Sift flour into a bowl, stir in oat bran. Add eggs, stir until mixture is smooth. Gradually stir in milk, mix to a smooth batter. Cover and stand for about 30 minutes.

Transfer batter to a small jug. Heat a small, heavy-based frying pan, grease well. Pour 2 to 3 tablespoons of batter into pan, swirl batter evenly over base of pan, cook until underside is golden brown. Toss or turn pancake, cook on other side. Repeat with remaining batter.

Divide pancakes into 3 equal portions. Place one portion of pancakes over base of a greased 8-cup capacity ovenproof dish, cover with half of the filling, another portion of pancakes, then with remaining filling. Top with remaining pancakes, spread evenly with sauce, sprinkle with parmesan cheese. Bake in moderate oven for about 30 minutes or until lasagne is lightly browned.

Filling

Melt butter in a large frying pan, add garlic and onion, stir over heat until onion is soft, or microwave on high 2 minutes. Add celery, zucchini, pumpkin, undrained crushed tomatoes and baked beans, stir over heat until mixture boils, then reduce heat and simmer, uncovered for about 30 minutes or until most of the liquid has evaporated and mixture is thick.

Sauce

Melt butter in small saucepan or microwave on high 30 seconds, add flour and oat bran, stir over heat for 1 minute or microwave on high 1 minute. Gradually add milk, stir until mixture boils and thickens, or microwave on high 3 minutes. Serves 6.

PUMPKIN AND VEGETABLE CURRY

1 large vegetable stock cube, crumbled

1 tablespoon polyunsaturated oil	500g baby potatoes
1 onion, chopped	350g pumpkin, chopped
1-1/2 tablespoons plain flour	250g broccoli, chopped
1 tablespoon curry powder	1 teaspoon cumin seeds
2 teaspoons chilli sauce	2 cups water

Heat oil in a medium saucepan, add onion, stir over medium heat for about 2 minutes, or microwave on high for about 3 minutes, or until onion is soft. Add flour, curry, sauce and cumin, stir over medium heat for 1 minute, or microwave on high for 1 minute.

Remove saucepan from heat, gradually stir in combined water and stock cube, stir over high heat, or microwave on high for about 4 minutes, until mixture boils and thickens. Reduce heat, add potatoes, simmer, partly covered, for about 20 minutes, or microwave on high for about 15 minutes, or until the potatoes are almost cooked, stirring occasionally.

Add pumpkin & broccoli, simmer for a further 10 minutes, or microwave on high for about 3 minutes, or until broccoli is just soft. Transfer curry to serving dish. Serves 4.

19

SAVOURY PUMPKIN PATTIES

2 cups cooked, mashed pumpkin
1 medium brown onion finely chopped
1 clove garlic, crushed
1 long stick celery, finely chopped
150g sharp cheese, grated
1 teaspoon salt
1/2 cup wholemeal plain flour

1 cup rolled oats
1/2 cup soy flour
1/2 cup gluten flour
oil for frying

Combine all the patty ingredients. Mix well. Drop the mixture a spoon at a time into hot oil and fry gently until crisp and brown on the outside. If preferred, you can give the patties more even shapes by dropping them into more flour and rolling them between the floured palms of your hands before frying.

SWEET AND SOUR PUMPKIN

vegetable oil for shallow frying
575g yellow pumpkin, skinned, seeded and thinly sliced
3 to 4 tablespoons wine vinegar
25g sugar
1 tablespoon chopped mint
2 garlic cloves, peeled and crushed
salt and pepper

Heat the oil 5 mm deep in a large frying pan. Add the pumpkin slices and fry until golden brown on both sides. Drain off most of the oil from the pan, then add the vinegar, sugar, mint, garlic and salt and pepper to taste. Cook for a further 10 minutes, turning the pumpkin slices over halfway through cooking. Serve immediately. Serves 4.

MEDITERRANEAN PUMPKIN BEEF AND CHICKEN

2 tablespoons olive oil
450g chuck steak, cubed
1 medium chicken, cut in pieces
4 medium onions, thinly sliced
420g canned whole tomatoes
1 bunch parsley
1 bunch coriander
1-1/2 litres water to cover the meat
1 small cabbage, quartered
500g pumpkin, cubed
4 zucchini, unpeeled and cut into sticks
4 medium turnips, peeled and quartered

salt and pepper
1/2 teaspoon saffron
2 teaspoons turmeric
2 teaspoons ground ginger
4 medium carrots
420g can chick peas
775g couscous
110g butter
50g raisins
4 celery stalks

Heat the oil in the bottom part of a steamer and brown the beef and chicken. Add the chopped onions and cook until soft.

Add the tomatoes and bring to a rolling boil. Wash the parsley and coriander under running water, tie together with string and add to the broth. Add the water, turnips, celery, carrots and spices.

Cover tightly and boil until the chicken is tender, about 1-1/2 hours. Remove the chicken, turnips, celery and carrots from the broth and keep them warm in a covered dish in the oven. Leave the beef in the broth. Add the pumpkin and cabbage and simmer until the pumpkin is tender, about 45 minutes. Remove the pumpkin, cabbage and beef from the broth, and keep them warm in another covered dish in the oven.

Add the zucchini to the broth and simmer until tender, about 15 minutes. Remove the zucchini and add to the other vegetables in the oven. Discard the parsley and coriander, and leave the broth in the steamer.

Rinse the couscous under running water. Bring the

broth to a rolling boil in the bottom of the steamer. Spread a cupful of couscous in the steamer section and cook until the grain becomes plump and tender, about 15 minutes. Place the steamed couscous in a covered pan and keep warm in the oven. Repeat this process until all the couscous has been steamed.

Mix the steamed couscous with 115ml broth and 4 tablespoons butter. Fluff with a fork to separate the grains. Cover with foil and keep warm until serving time.

To serve, reheat the broth, adding the chick peas. Spread the cooked couscous grain on a large platter. Place the chicken and the beef in the centre of the couscous and arrange the vegetables around the meat. Ladle a little broth over the entire dish and sprinkle with raisins.

Set the platter in the centre of the table and let your guests serve themselves.

Serve the extra broth in a bowl on the side. Serves 8.

PUMPKIN APPLE FRITTERS

1 apple
1/2 cup cold mashed pumpkin
sugar to taste
1/2 teaspoon ground cinnamon
1/4 teaspoon nutmeg
2/3 cup skim milk powder
1/2 teaspoon almond essence

Core and grate apple. Combine with remaining ingredients in bowl. Drop by teaspoonfuls on non-stick baking sheet coated with vegetable cooking spray. Flatten with back of spoon. Bake in 375F oven for 20 minutes.

Combine 1 teaspoon cinnamon with a little sugar. Sprinkle over apple pumpkin thins. Serve warm. Serves two.

CURRY PUMPKIN & POTATO

Take some cold meat (remove skin, fat and gristle), mince and season with pepper, salt and curry powder. Mash some potatoes and pumpkin with an egg; season with pepper and salt. Line patty tins with potato and pumpkin; fill with meat; cover with potatoes and pumpkin again, orna- ment the edges, brush with milk and bake in quick oven.

PUMPKIN QUICHE

1/2 cup wholemeal self-raising flour
1/2 cup wholemeal plain flour
125g butter
1 egg yolk
2 teaspoons lemon juice, approximately

Filling

500g pumpkin	3 eggs
2 rashers bacon	2/3 cup cream
3 shallots	2 tablespoons chopped parsley
1 clove garlic	pepper
250g feta cheese	

Sift flours into basin, return husks from sifter to basin, rub in butter, add egg yolk and enough lemon juice to just combine ingredients. Cover, refrigerate 30 minutes. Roll pastry to fit 23cm flan tin, bake in moderately hot oven 10 minutes. Pour in filling, bake in moderate oven further 30 minutes or until set.

Filling:

Peel pumpkin, boil or steam until tender, drain well, cool. Chop bacon finely, cook in pan until crisp, add chopped shallots and crushed garlic, cook few minutes. Push cheese and pumpkin through sieve, add lightly beaten eggs, cream, parsley and pepper, mix well, add bacon mix- ture.

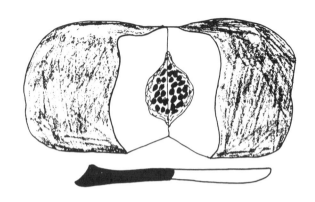

PUMPKIN CROQUETTES

2 cups dry mashed pumpkin
1 tablespoon finely chopped mint
1 tablespoon milk
1 dessertspoon butter/margarine

1 egg (separated)
salt and pepper
1 cup cooked peas
bread crumbs

Add milk, butter and egg yolk to pumpkin, beat until smooth. Season with mint, salt and pepper. Form the mixture into small balls, scoop out the centres and fill each with a dessertspoon of peas. Fill the hole with a little more pumpkin and re-shape the balls.

Lightly beat the egg white and roll the pumpkin balls first in the egg white, then in the breadcrumbs. Refrigerate until firm. Fry in deep fat until golden brown. Drain on absorbent paper.

GLAZED PUMPKIN

Cut pumpkin into thin slices and brush with oil, arrange in greased casserole dish. Pour over thin layer of dark corn syrup, sprinkle with nutmeg.

Bake in moderately hot oven until pumpkin is tender when tested with a skewer. Serve with a roast and other vegetables.

PUMPKIN WITH PARMESAN CHEESE

Peel a 1-1/2 kilo section of pumpkin and discard the seeds with the loose cotton surrounding them. Cut the firm part into square pieces and parboil them in salted water. Do not cook them completely, or they will start to disintegrate. Fry them in clarified butter on both sides, scattering them with salt, nutmeg and cinnamon. As they become lightly coloured, remove the squares to a serving dish, piling them up in the centre. Cover them with grated parmesan cheese, and bake in a hot oven until the cheese is nicely golden. Parmesan cheese can be eked out with dry cheddar.

RICH BAKED PUMPKIN

1 pumpkin
3 cups well cooked soy beans, mashed or 3 cups cooked brown lentils
2 onions
250g mushrooms, washed and sliced
freshly chopped parsley
soy sauce
1 cup fresh wholemeal breadcrumbs
dried sweet basil
tahini

Wash the pumpkin thoroughly and place on a tray. Bake at 300F or 160C until the pumpkin feels slightly tender when pressed. (For a 3kg pumpkin, you will probably need to bake it for 2-1/2 to 3 hours).

When cooked, use a sharp knife to cut a circle around the stalk and core of pumpkin. Lift up this lid by holding onto the stalk as a handle. Using a long-handled spoon, carefully scoop out the seeds. Mix the remaining ingredients thoroughly and use for stuffing the pumpkin. Reheat the pumpkin at 350F or 180C for 20 minutes. Serve cut in wedges.

PUMPKIN VICHYSSOISE

750g pumpkin
2 leeks or 2 large onions
250g potatoes

2 large or 4 small chicken stock cubes
250ml cream
salt and pepper

Prepare vegetables and boil in water with chicken cubes until very soft. Push through sieve. Return to saucepan, add cream, salt and pepper and reheat. Serve hot or chilled.

STEAMED PUMPKIN & VEGETABLES

500g pumpkin, washed, seeded, cut in chunks (skin on)
2 medium carrots, washed, cut in chunks
2 medium zucchini, washed, cut in chunks
1 red capsicum, washed, cut in strips
1 cup tiny broccoli flowerets or cauliflowerlets
freshly chopped parsley

Place vegetables in steamer in order mentioned, leaving out the broccoli or cauliflower and capsicum until the last 5 minutes of cooking. Steam until just tender. Delicious served at once, or as a salad.

PUMPKIN STOCKPOT

1 oz butter
500g pumpkin
2 medium potatoes
3 large carrots, chopped
2 pints chicken stock
1 level tablespoon tomato paste

2 oz pasta shapes
1 tablespoon parsley
4 oz grated cheese
1 large onion chopped
1 medium turnip
4 sticks celery

Heat butter in large pan, add vegetables and saute 5 minutes. Add stock, seasoning and tomato paste. Bring to boil and simmer 45 minutes until vegetables are tender. Add pasta and cook 15 minutes. Serve sprinkled with cheese and parsley.

PUMPKIN PATTIES

1 cup pureed, cooked pumpkin
1 egg, lightly beaten
2 dessertspoons tahini
1 small onion, finely chopped
1 clove garlic

1/2 cup wholemeal flour
1/2 cup rolled oats
salt and cayenne pepper
nutmeg
breadcrumbs

Put pumpkin in a bowl, whisk in the beaten egg. Stir in onion, garlic, parsley and tahini. Sift together the flour and spices, mix in well. Sprinkle breadcrumbs over greaseproof paper, drop rounded tablespoons of pumpkin mixture onto crumbs. Toss in crumbs, flatten into cakes. Lower into hot oil and fry until golden brown.

PUMPKIN PRATIES

8 large potatoes
2 cups cooked, mashed pumpkin
salt and freshly ground black pepper
1-2 tablespoons hot milk
1/4 cup finely grated parmesan cheese

Bake potatoes in the oven in their jackets. Remove from the oven and cut a 2 cm slice lengthwise from each. Scoop out the centre and peel away the skin from the top.

Put scooped out potato in a small saucepan and mash well. Add pumpkin, salt and pepper to taste and a little hot milk, if needed, to make a smooth piping consistency.

Place mixture in a piping bag and pipe back into the potato shells. Sprinkle with cheese and grill until tops are golden brown. Serve immediately.

BRAISED PUMPKIN & BEEF

900g Top rump of beef   salt and pepper
1 onion   600g pumpkin
2 tablespoons oil   90ml dry white wine
150ml beef stock

Preheat the oven to 170C.
Tie the meat into a neat shape with fine string. Peel and thinly slice the onion. Heat the oil in a flameproof casserole, add onion and fry till transparent. Add the meat and fry over a high heat till browned all over.

Add the stock and seasoning, cover and cook in the oven for 1 hour.

Meanwhile, to prepare the pumpkin, scrape out the seeds and fibrous centre. Remove the skin and cut the flesh into chunks. Add to the casserole with the wine. Cover and cook for a further 1 hour till the meat is tender. Taste and adjust the seasoning.

Remove the string, slice the meat thickly and arrange in a warmed serving dish. Arrange the pumpkin around meat and spoon juices over. Serve immediately with creamed potatoes and a green vegetable.

Overall timing: 2-1/2 hours. Not suitable for freezing.

PUMPKIN FRITTERS

1 beaten egg   1 teaspoon baking powder
little milk   fat or oil for frying
2 cups cooked mashed pumpkin   salt and pepper
1 cup plain flour   1/2 teaspoon dry mustard

Sift dry ingredients into bowl. Add egg and pumpkin and a little milk if too dry. Heat oil in frying pan and then drop mixture by the tablespoonful. Cook each side until brown and crisp. Drain on absorbent paper and serve at once.

PUMPKIN HOTPOT

1 carrot, scrubbed, trimmed, chopped
1 large onion, chopped
1 leek, washed and sliced
1kg pumpkin with skin, washed, chopped into chunks
5 cups stock
1 bay leaf   a dash of soy sauce
2 cups milk   toasted cashews
salt and pepper   a little chopped parsley

Place pumpkin, carrot, onion and leeks in the saucepan with bay leaf and stock or water. Bring to the boil, reduce heat and cook gently 25-30 minutes, until vegetables have become soft.

Stir in milk and gently reheat. Remove bay leaf and if liked, blend until smooth. Season to taste with salt, soy sauce and pepper. Serve topped with toasted cashews and a dash of finely chopped parsley.

SAVOURY PUMPKIN

8 slices butternut pumpkin, cut from end without pips
1 onion, chopped
1 teaspoon oil
2 cups cooked rice
2 cups grated cheddar cheese
Any of the following, chopped and mixed together: Olives, herbs, mushrooms, tomatoes.

Bake pumpkin slices on greased baking tray at 200C (400F) until soft.

Meanwhile, cook onion in oil until soft but not coloured (about 5 minutes). When onion is soft add cooked rice and other ingredients but reserve 1 cup of grated cheese.

Pile mixture onto pumpkin slices and sprinkle with remaining cheese.

Bake in oven for further 10 minutes. Serves 4 to 6.

PUMPKIN AU-GRATIN

2 cups diced, just cooked pumpkin (still firm).

Make a white sauce, add plenty of grated cheese, some chopped chives and parsley (or celery leaves). Season according to taste and pour sauce over pumpkin pieces in a casserole dish. Sprinkle with breadcrumbs, dot with butter and bake about 15 minutes in a moderate oven.

PUMPKIN CUTLETS

tablespoon oil
1 teaspoon mixed herbs
1/4 teaspoon ground ginger
2 large eggs
250g raw unsalted cashew nut pieces
250g raw unsalted brazil nut pieces
150g mild cheddar cheese
1/2 cup wheat germ
500g cauliflower
750g butternut pumpkin, peeled, seeded and cut into large chunks
1 small eggplant, peeled, quartered
2 small zucchinis, scrubbed and ends trimmed
1 large onion, peeled and diced

Steam all the vegetables until tender. Saute the onion in oil in a frypan until light golden. Mash all the steamed vegetables and mix in the onion, herbs and ginger.

Beat the eggs and mix into the vegetables with the nuts and cheese. Form mixture into desired shapes.

Roll each cutlet in wheat germ and place them on a well-oiled tray. Bake the cutlets in the oven for 5 minutes at 175C, then reduce to 150C for a further 15-20 minutes, depending on the size of the cutlets.

Serve with hot steamed vegetables, such as peas or beans with broccoli, or with a freshly made salad. Serves 6.

PUMPKIN AU VIN

4 cups pumpkin chopped into 2 cm cubes (no need to peel)
500g fresh or tinned tomatoes   1 onion, chopped
1 tablespoon cooking sherry or port   1 teaspoon oil
1 teaspoon oregano

Cook onion in oil until soft but not coloured (about 5 minutes).

Add tomatoes, sherry and pumpkin cubes and simmer uncovered, stirring occasionally. When pumpkin is softening add oregano. Cook until pumpkin is very soft, but not disintegrated.

Serve over boiled rice and sprinkle with grated cheese. Serves 4.

STUFFED BUTTERNUT PUMPKIN

1 medium butternut pumpkin, washed
salt, pepper   2 cloves garlic, crushed
500g soft ricotta cheese   dash of soy sauce
1-1/2 cups walnut pieces   a swirl of tahini

Cut pumpkin in half and remove pips with a spoon. Sprinkle with salt and pepper. Place on a greased baking tray and bake at 350F (180C) for about 50 minutes, or just tender.

Mix the remaining ingredients thoroughly. Pile into cavities of baked butternut. Reheat at 350F or 180C for about 15 minutes. Sprinkle with parsley and serve at once. Serves 4 to 6.

BAKED SESAME PUMPKIN

750g pumpkin, washed, seeded   oil
1 red capsicum, seeded, cut in rings   pepper
Handful of sesame seeds   sweet paprika
A few chopped spring onions or 1 small onion, cut in fine rings

Slice pumpkin (skin on) about 1 cm thick. Arrange on baking tray and sprinkle with a little oil. Top with onion rings, sesame seeds and a little black pepper. Bake in a moderate oven for about 20 minutes. Remove from oven and top with capsicum and a shaking of paprika. Continue baking until pumpkin is tender, about 5 to 10 minutes.

Serve hot or cold. Serves 6.

PUMPKIN & CORN HOTPOT

150g fresh mushrooms, diced
2 tablespoons raw tahini (sesame butter)
500g peas   2 tablespoons chopped chives
4 cobs young sweet corn   2 medium onions, diced
600g butternut pumpkin   1/4 teaspoon ground ginger
3 medium carrots, scrubbed   1 tablespoon oil

Steam the corn cobs until the kernels are tender, about 15 minutes. Remove the corn; steam pumpkin, carrots, and peas. Meanwhile, cut the corn kernels from the cobs, taking care to remove the entire kernel, especially the tiny germ at the head.
Put the kernels in a small bowl and mix them with the tahini and chives.
As the other vegetables become just tender, remove them from the steamer. Meanwhile saute the onions in the oil until tender, then add the mushrooms and ginger and saute a further 5 minutes.

Cut the skin from the pumpkin (if wished) and dice or slice as preferred. Slice the carrots. Place layers of vegetables into a casserole dish, with corn mixture forming a centre layer and the onion mixture poured over the top.

Cover the casserole dish and put it in the oven until the casserole is thoroughly heated through (about 15 minutes). Serve hot from the oven. Serves 4.

PUMPKIN SEED SALAD

1 large or 2 small avocados
200g fresh small mushrooms
200g pumpkin seed kernels (pepitas)
1/2 cup fresh alfalfa sprouts
1/2 cup fresh lentil sprouts
2 large tomatoes, cut into chunks
2 stalks celery, chopped
4 large lettuce leaves, torn into small pieces
1 red capsicum, cored and diced
1 raw beetroot, scrubbed and grated

Peel the avocado and cut into chunks. Wash the mushrooms, remove the stalks, and cut the caps into chunks. If desired, grind pepitas into a coarse meal, or leave whole if everyone has good teeth. Mix all the ingredients together in a large serving bowl.

PUMPKIN SPRING SALAD

250g pumpkin, chopped
425g can baby corn, drained and chopped
250g baby squash, halved
300g cauliflower, chopped
300g beans, chopped
Warm vinaigrette
1/4 cup polyunsaturated oil
1 onion, sliced
2 small fresh red chillies
1 teaspoon poppy seeds
1/2 teaspoon yellow mustard seeds
1/2 teaspoon black mustard seeds
1/4 cup lemon juice

Boil, steam or microwave vegetables until just soft; drain. Combine warm vegetables on a large serving plate, pour warm vinaigrette over top; serve salad warm.

Warm vinaigrette

Heat the oil in a small saucepan, add onion, stir over medium heat for 3 minutes, or until onion is soft. Add choppped chillies, poppy and mustard seeds, stir over medium heat for about 3 minutes, or until seeds begin to pop; stir in lemon juice. Serve immediately. Serves 4.

PUMPKIN SUMMER SALAD

250g fresh mushrooms, chopped finely
250g butternut pumpkin
250g raw cashew nut pieces
4 tablespoons raw tahini (sesame butter)
1 large tomato, diced finely
250g blanched almond pieces
1 long thin green cucumber, sliced thinly
2 stalks celery, chopped finely
1 medium sized red capsicum, cored and diced finely

Steam the pumpkin until tender, then mash it thoroughly.

Mix the tahini, tomato, and pumpkin together and mash thoroughly. Add the nuts, mushrooms, celery and capsicum to this mixture and again mix thoroughly.

Line the inside of a bowl (desirably glass) as completely as possible with sliced cucumber. Place the mixture into bowl and press it down firmly. Refrigerate until cold.

To serve, ease the salad out of the bowl like a firm jelly from a mould. Then place it in the centre of the table and surround it with a variety of other vegetables. Serves 6.

SCRUMPTIOUS PUMPKIN PIE

Pie shell

100g plain flour	3 tablespoons cold water
2 tablespoons cold butter	pinch salt

Filling

1 small pumpkin (about 500g)	1/4 teaspoon ground cloves
2 eggs	1/2 teaspoon ground ginger
30g butter	1/2 teaspoon nutmeg
200g sugar	1/2 teaspoon cinnamon
50ml molasses or golden syrup	100ml milk
1 tablespoon cornflour	salt

Cut the butter into the flour until it is in pieces about the size of a pea. Rub the butter into the flour with the fingers. Add the water and mix the dough thoroughly by hand. Roll the dough out on a floured board and use it to line a 20cm pie dish.

Peel the pumpkin and remove the seeds. Boil it and discard the water. Mash the boiled pumpkin and add to it the melted butter, beaten eggs, molasses, sugar, flour, milk, salt and spices. Mix thoroughly. Fill the pie casing with the pumpkin mixture and bake in a moderate oven for an hour. Serve hot or cold, with or without cream.

PUMPKIN PEDESTAL PIES

Pie crust
1/4 cup water

1/4 cup melted butter
sifter full of flour

Mix all ingredients until right consistency for pastry dough. Roll out thinly and lay bottom of pie plate down on rolled out dough and cut around. Lift the dough up from underneath and place in the bottom of pie plate. Should make 2 to 3 crusts depending on desired thickness.

Filling
3 cups cooked mashed pumpkin
1 cup sugar
1 egg
1 heaped teaspoon cinnamon

1 teaspoon ginger
salt to taste
2 tablespoons flour

Pour mixture into pie shells. If desired, sprinkle more cinnamon and ginger on top. Cook in moderately slow oven for 15 minutes or until done.

SMOKEY PUMPKIN PIES

375g packet prepared short crust
  or puff pastry
2 rashers bacon, finely chopped
1 small onion, finely chopped
250g cold mashed pumpkin
125g Australian smoked processed cheddar cheese, coarsely grated

3 eggs, separated
2 tablespoons milk
1 teaspoon salt
pepper

Roll out pastry to 3mm thickness. Using a 9cm pastry cutter, cut circles and press into 6cm diameter patty pans. Blend all remaining ingredients together except for egg whites. Beat reserved egg whites until stiff peaks form. Fold into filling mixture. Spoon into pastry lined patty pans. Top each with a small piece of bacon if desired. Bake at 230C for 10 minutes. Reduce oven to 190C. Bake a further 15 minutes or until golden brown. Makes approximately 18-20.

PYGMY PUMPKIN PIES

2 tablespoons chopped fresh parsley
2 teaspoons hot water
1/2 vegetable stock cube, crumbled
4 sheets wholemeal shortcrust pastry
1 egg lightly beaten, extra
2 tablespoons sunflower kernels

750g pumpkin, peeled
1 egg, lightly beaten
1/2 cup bran flakes
30g margerine
1 leek, sliced

Grease 8 holes of a large muffin pan. Boil, steam or microwave pumpkin until tender; drain well.

Blend or process pumpkin until smooth, add egg and bran flakes; mix well. Melt margarine in a medium frying pan, add leek, stir over medium heat for about 5 minutes, or microwave on high for about 3 minutes, or until soft. Combine parsley, leek, hot water and stock cube; stir into pumpkin mixture; mix well.

Using an 11cm plain cutter, cut 8 rounds from 2 sheets of the pastry. Using an 8cm plain cutter, cut out 8 rounds from remaining pastry. Line base and sides of prepared pan with large pastry rounds, fill evenly with pumpkin mixture. Brush pastry edges with extra egg, top with remaining rounds of pastry. Brush pie tops with extra egg and sprinkle with sunflower kernels. Bake in moderately hot oven about 40 minutes, or until golden. Makes 8.

MACROBIOTIC PUMPKIN PIE

900g pumpkin, peeled and cut into 2.5cm cubes
1 cup water
pinch of salt
1 beaten egg
1/2 cup fruit juice

1 egg yolk, beaten
1 medium pie shell
1 teaspoon cinnamon

Pre-heat oven to 450F (235C). Boil the pumpkin in water until tender. Drain and mash by hand or in a blender. Stir in remaining ingredients except egg yolk, and pour into a pie dish. Cover with pastry top, brush with egg yolk and bake for 30 to 40 minutes.

PUMPKIN PIE WITH PECAN TOFFEE TOPPING

Pastry
90g butter
2 tablespoons castor sugar
1 egg, lightly beaten
1 cup plain flour
1/4 cup self-raising flour
1/4 cup cornflour

Pecan toffee
1/2 cup castor sugar
1/3 cup dark corn syrup
50g butter
1/2 cup pecans

Filling
1 cup cooked mashed pumpkin
150ml can evaporated milk
2 eggs, lightly beaten
1/2 cup cream
1/3 cup brown sugar
1-1/2 tablespoons plain flour
1/2 teaspoon ground cinnamon
1/2 teaspoon ground nutmeg

Filling

Combine pumpkin, milk, eggs, cream, sugar, sifted flour and spices in a large bowl; beat gently until smooth.

Pastry

Cream butter and sugar in a small bowl with electric mixer until light and fluffy, beat in egg, beat until just combined. Stir in sifted flours, mix to a soft dough. Gently knead dough on a lightly floured surface until smooth; cover and refrigerate for 15 minutes.

Place pastry dough between 2 sheets of paper, roll out pastry until large enough to line a 23cm pie dish. Remove paper, gently ease pastry into dish, trim edge of pastry, cover and refrigerate 15 minutes.

Place paper over pastry, cover with dried beans or rice. Bake in moderately hot oven for 5 minutes, remove paper and beans, bake pastry for a further 10 minutes, or until lightly browned. Cool to room temperature.

Pour filling into pie crust, bake in moderate oven for about 45 minutes, or until filling is set. Let pie stand for 30 minutes, then quickly spread pecan toffee over filling. Refrigerate for about 20 minutes, or until toffee is just firm.

Pecan toffee

Combine the sugar, corn syrup and butter in a small heavy-based saucepan, stir constantly over medium heat, without boiling, until sugar is dissolved; stir in nuts. Bring to the boil, then boil uncovered and without stirring for about 4 minutes, or until golden brown. Remove from heat.

SWEET PUMPKIN PIE

1 kg pumpkin
1-1/2 cups sultanas or currants
1-1/2 cups plain wholemeal flour
3 tablespoons butter or margarine
1 tablespoon honey
1 teaspoon ground cinnamon
1 tablespoon oil or tahini
1/2 to 2/3 cups water
1 tablespoon ground cinnamon
1 teaspoon mixed spice
3 tablespoons arrowroot

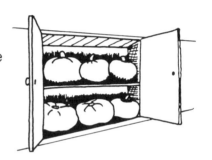

Sift flour into mixing bowl. Melt butter or margarine gently. Add honey and ground cinnamon to melted butter.

Make a well in the centre and add the butter or margarine and the oil. Gradually add a little water to the well and mix quickly using your hand until a soft dough consistency is obtained. Knead lightly. Roll out pastry and line a 10 inch quiche or pie tin. Trim edges.

Steam pumpkin until very tender (about 15 minutes). Blend until smooth with honey and spices adding arrowroot quickly while blender is in operation. Add sultanas or currants. Cool slightly. Pour mixture into pastry case and bake at once at 375F or 190C for 30 minutes. Cool and chill.

Serve topped with whipped cream or yoghurt and a dusting of cinnamon.

GINGER PUMPKIN PIE

Pastry
1 cup wholemeal plain flour
1/2 cup wholemeal self-raising flour

1/4 teaspoon nutmeg
1/4 teaspoon mixed spice
2 tablespoons raw sugar
pinch vegetable salt
2 tablespoons sesame seeds
125g margarine
1 egg yolk
2 tablespoons water
extra nutmeg

Filling
2 eggs
3/4 cup plain thick yoghurt
1 teaspoon ground ginger
1/2 teaspoon cinnamon
1/4 teaspoon mixed spice
1/4 cup honey
750g pumpkin

Pastry

Sift flours, nutmeg, mixed spice and salt into bowl, return any husks in sifter to bowl. Add sesame seeds and sugar; mix lightly. Rub in margarine until mixture resembles fine bread-crumbs. Add egg yolk and water; mix to a firm dough. Turn out on to lightly floured surface; knead lightly.

Roll out pastry to cover base and sides of 23cm pie plate. Decorate edges. Refrigerate 30 minutes. Cook in moderate oven 12 to 15 minutes or until light golden brown. Remove from oven, allow to become cold.

When cold, spoon in prepared filling. Sprinkle with extra nutmeg. Return to moderate oven, cook further 35 to 40 minutes or until filling has set. Allow pie to cool, then refrigerate until cold.

Filling

Remove seeds from pumpkin, cut pumpkin into pieces, remove skin. Place pumpkin in boiling salted water, cover, reduce heat, simmer 20 minutes or until pumpkin is tender; drain well. Push pumpkin through fine sieve. You will need 1-1/2 cups pumpkin.

Place eggs, ginger, cinnamon, mixed spice, honey and yoghurt in bowl; whisk well. Add pumpkin, mix well.

BLUE PUMPKIN PIE

3 large eggs
500g Queensland blue pumpkin
1-1/2 cups raw wheat germ
3/4 cup desiccated coconut
3 tablespoons vegetable oil
3 tablespoons raw cashew butter
150g seeded raisins
1/2 cup water
4 tablespoons instant soya milk powder
1 teaspoon ground cinnamon
4 tablespoons maple syrup

Soak the raisins in the water for 2 hours. Cut the pumpkin into large pieces, retaining the skin, and steam until tender. Meanwhile, pour the wheat germ and coconut into a large mixing bowl.

In a smaller mixing bowl, pour the oil and cashew butter, and thoroughly mix them. Pour the oil-cashew mixture into the larger mixing bowl and mix thoroughly with wheatgerm and coconut, working them together with the fingers.

Brush a little oil around the inside of a 23cm shallow pie dish. Line the inside of the pie dish with the crust mixture, packing it flat and evenly against sides and bottom.

Peel the pumpkin, cut into chunks, and put in the blender jug. Add the water and raisins, oil, soya milk powder, maple syrup, eggs and cinnamon to the blender and blend at three-quarters of full speed until smooth.

Pour the blended liquid into the pie crust, smooth it and place in the oven. Bake at 175C (345F) until set (when inserted knife can be withdrawn clean); this usually requires 40 to 50 minutes baking time. Setting will continue after it has been taken out of the oven. This pie should be served cold.

FRUITY PUMPKIN PIE

185g butter
1 egg yolk
2 tablespoons water, approximately

2 cups plain flour
1 tablespoon icing sugar

Filling
2 cups mashed pumpkin (not butternut pumpkin)
1/2 cup brown sugar, firmly packed
1 tablespoon treacle or golden syrup
2 teaspoons mixed spice
2 teaspoons cinnamon
2/3 cup sultanas

1/3 cup currants
1/3 cup mixed peel

Sift dry ingredients into basin, rub in butter, add egg yolk and enough water to mix to a firm, pliable dough. Wrap in plastic food wrap, refrigerate 30 minutes. Roll two thirds of pastry to line base and sides of 18cm pie plate, spread with filling, top with remaining pastry; trim and decorate.

Bake in moderately hot oven 10 minutes, reduce heat to moderate, bake further 20 to 30 minutes or until golden brown. Cool to room temperature before serving. Serve with cream.

Filling:
Combine pumpkin with sugar, treacle, spices and fruits, mix well.

PUMPKIN AND CHEESE PIE

1 kg pumpkin, steamed then mashed
1/2 cup cream or evaporated milk
extra cheese to sprinkle on top
3 tablespoons cooked rice

2 tablespoons butter
salt and pepper
2 eggs, beaten
60g grated tasty cheese

Mix all ingredients well together. Pour into greased casserole dish. Sprinkle with extra grated cheese and dot with butter. Bake in moderate oven about 30 minutes or until browned.

PUMPKIN CUSTARD PIE

1/4 cup cold water
1/2 cup sugar
1/4 cup powdered milk
1 cup fresh milk
1 cup steamed and mashed pumpkin
3 tablespoons dark molasses
1/2 teaspoon each ginger and cinnamon
1/2 cup chilled natural lard or 2/3 cup partially hardened

margarine or butter
3 eggs, separated
1/4 teaspoon salt
3/4 cup plain flour
1 teaspoon salt
1/2 cup wheat germ

Sift flour and 1 teaspoon salt into mixing bowl. Add wheat germ and stir well.

Cut lard or margarine or butter into dry ingredients with pastry cutter or two knives until particles of fat are the size of large peas; do not touch with hands.

Add cold water; mix only enough to moisten ingredients. Turn dough onto floured surface; knead just enough to hold dough together. Pat dough quickly into a flat, round ball, dust top lightly with flour, and roll 3mm thick, using a circular motion of the rolling pin to give a perfect circle of dough.

Use dough to line a 23cm pie shell; trim and flute edges and make perforations with a fork at 2 inch intervals. If time permits, chill in refrigerator or freeze before baking. Bake in hot oven for 8 to 10 minutes.

Combine sugar and powdered milk. Stir well; add fresh milk, egg yolks, pumpkin, molasses, ginger, cinnamon and salt. Beat egg whites until stiff; fold into custard just before baking.

Take baked pie shell from oven; slip shell onto serving plate; grease the pan generously and pour custard into it.

Lower oven temperature to 325 F; bake custard 25 to 30 minutes, or until barely firm; cooking will continue as custard cools.

Immediately before serving, loosen custard with spatula

43

or knife; slip carefully into crust. The crust can become soggy about 30 minutes after the custard is put into it; combine the two just before pie is to be eaten.

TRADITIONAL PUMPKIN PIE

1 x 23cm unbaked pie shell
1 cup sugar
2 tablespoons flour
1/2 teaspoon each of cinnamon, nutmeg,
ground ginger, cloves and salt
3 eggs
1-1/2 cups mashed pumpkin
2 cups milk or 1 cup evaporated milk and 1 cup water
whipped cream to decorate

Mix together all dry ingredients. Beat in eggs. Stir in pumpkin and milk. Pour into pie shell and bake 45-50 minutes in a hot oven. Cool and serve with whipped cream and sprinkle with nutmeg.

PUMPKIN PIE

23cm unbaked pastry shell
2 cups cooked pumpkin
2 eggs
1/2 cup castor sugar·
1 tablespoon flour
1 teaspoon cinnamon
1/2 teaspoon salt
1/4 teaspoon ground ginger
1/4 teaspoon nutmeg
1 cup instant full cream milk powder
1/2 cup reduced cream

Prepare pastry shell but leave uncooked. Mash pumpkin until smooth and push through a sieve to remove all fibre. Beat in remaining ingredients and spoon into uncooked pastry shell. Bake in a 200C oven for 15 minutes. Reduce heat to 180C and bake further 40 minutes or until cooked through. Cool a little, sprinkle with icing sugar and serve warm. Serves 6.

AUSTRALIAN PUMPKIN PIE

pumpkin
6 eggs
3 pints milk

flavouring of mace
nutmeg or lemon as preferred

Pare the pumpkin, take out the seeds, and stew until soft. Press through a sieve, and to each quart of the pulp allow the ingredients named above. Mix with the pulp first the sugar, then the yolks and whites of the eggs, beaten separately, and the flavouring, and beat all together. Line the rim of a buttered dish with puff paste, pour in the mixture, and bake in a rather quick oven.
Bake for 3/4 hour.

MOUTH-WATERING PUMPKIN ICE CREAM

1/2 cup cooked mashed pumpkin
1/4 cup milk
50g brown sugar
pinch salt

1/2 teaspoon cinnamon
1/4 teaspoon ginger
1/2 teaspoon vanilla essence
1 cup cream, whipped

Combine all ingredients except cream. Fold the mixture slowly into whipped cream. Pour into a shallow metal dish and freeze to the desired consistency. Makes 500ml.

PUMPKIN-PIE PUDDING

500g pumpkin, steamed and mashed   1/2 cup skim milk
1/2 teaspoon each cinnamon and nutmeg 2 eggs, beaten
1/2 teaspoon ginger, or to taste   2 tablespoons honey
1/2 teaspoon vanilla essence
pinch salt

Combine all ingredients and spoon into 6 custard cups. Set cups in pan of hot water and bake in moderate oven 50 minutes, or until centres are set. Makes 6 servings.

PUMPKIN CUSTARD FLANS

1 cup cooked mashed pumpkin   **Pecan toffee**
200g sweetened condensed milk   60g butter
1 egg   1/2 cup brown sugar
1 tablespoon cornflour   1/4 cup golden syrup
1/2 teaspoon mixed spice   1/3 cup chopped pecan nuts
2 tablespoons brown sugar
2 tablespoons cold water

Blend pumpkin, milk, egg, cornflour, spice, sugar and water in bowl, stir until smooth. Pour into 4 (1/2 cup capacity) greased ovenproof dishes. Place dishes in baking tray with enough hot water to come halfway up sides of dishes.

Bake in moderate oven for 25 minutes or until set (or microwave on medium for about 8 minutes, stirring once halfway during cooking). Cover, refrigerate several hours or overnight. Serve with cream and chopped toffee.

Pecan toffee

Combine butter, sugar and syrup in saucepan, stir over heat without boiling until sugar is dissolved. Increase heat, boil rapidly for about 10 minutes or until mixture is golden brown. Spread pecans onto greased oven tray, pour toffee over pecans, cool.

PUMPKIN PUDDING

60ml water
1 tablespoon gelatine
60ml boiling water
120g cooked pumpkin
60g skim milk powder

1/4 teaspoon mixed spice
1/4 teaspoon maple syrup
1 tablespoon sugar
6 to 8 ice cubes

Pour water into blender goblet. Sprinkle gelatine over water to soften. Add boiling water. Blend about 30 seconds. Add all remaing ingredients except ice cubes and blend until smooth. Add ice cubes one at a time, blending after each addition, until all the cubes are used. Pour into dessert glasses. Serve immediately, or chill if desired. Makes 4 servings.

BAKED PUMPKIN CUSTARD

750g butternut pumpkin, seeds removed
1/2 cup water
1/2 cup maple syrup
1/2 teaspoon ground cinnamon

4 large eggs
500g ricotta cheese
1/2 teaspoon ground nutmeg

Steam the pumpkin until it is tender, then remove skin and mash. Into the blender place in order: water, maple syrup, cinnamon, pumpkin, eggs, and the ricotta cheese cut into pieces. Blend at three-quarters of full speed until smooth (about half a minute).

Pour into an open casserole dish and sprinkle nutmeg on top. Stand the dish in hot water in a larger tray. Bake at 150C (350F) until just set (about 1-1/4 hours). Serves 8.

PUMPKIN ICE-CREAM

1/4 teaspoon each salt, cinnamon, ginger and nutmeg
1-1/2 cups milk
2 cups cooked mashed pumpkin   3/4 cup brown sugar
2 eggs   1/2 cup cream

Mash or blend pumpkin until quite smooth. Beat in rest of ingredients. Pour into trays and freeze until starting to thicken and freeze around edges. Return ice-cream to bowl and beat until thick and creamy. Return to freezer.

Chopped glace ginger makes a fine garnish.

PUMPKIN PUDDING

1-1/3 cups cooked, mashed & drained pumpkin
1/4 cup packed brown sugar
1/4 teaspoon cinnamon   1-1/4 cups cold milk
1/4 teaspoon ginger   1 pkt vanilla instant pudding

Put all ingredients in blender and process until smooth. Pour into serving dishes and chill. Serve plain or with whipped cream. Serves 4.

PUMPKIN BREAD WITH SUNFLOWER SEEDS

400g butternut pumpkin, seeds removed
1/2 teaspoon vegetable salt (to control yeast in cooking dough)
1 cup cold water   3 tablespoons warm water
1 cup boiling water   1 sachet (7g) dry baker's yeast
1/2 cup buckwheat flour   1 tablespoon maple syrup
2 cups fine rice flour   75g raw sunflower seed kernels
1/2 cup fine millet meal   1 tablespoon oil (to oil bread tin)
1/2 cup fine corn meal   1 tablespoon hulled sesame seeds

Steam pumpkin until tender, then peel and mash until smooth in a large mixing bowl.

In the steaming saucepan, mix the corn meal, salt, and cold water until smooth. Slowly heat the mixture; add the boiling water and stir the mixture until thickened. Remove the corn meal from the heat and allow it to cool.

Mix the yeast, warm water, and maple syrup in a separate bowl until smooth. Allow the yeast mixture to stand until the yeast works into double size (about 10 minutes). Pour the yeast mixture, sunflower seeds, and corn meal into the mixing bowl containing the pumpkin. Mix thoroughly. Add all the flours to the mixture and continue to mix thoroughly for at least 5 minutes.

Evenly cover the inside of a bread tin with vegetable oil. Pack the dough into the bread tin, leaving a slight hollow in the centre. Lightly brush surface of dough with oil and sprinkle with sesame seeds.

Allow dough to stand for 40 to 45 minutes for initial rising to occur. Place in moderate oven and after 30 minutes reduce temperature to 175C (345F). Bake until the loaf is cooked through, for about another hour.

PUMPKIN BREAD WITH RAISINS AND NUTS

4 cups cooked mashed pumpkin
4 eggs, beaten
1 teaspoon vanilla
1 cup oil
4 cups sugar
2 teaspoons cinnamon
1 teaspoon cloves
1 teaspoon salt
4 teaspoons baking soda
5 cups flour
1 cup raisins
1 cup chopped nuts

In a large mixing bowl, using a wooden spoon combine pumpkin, eggs, vanilla, oil and sugar. Mix well. Sift together dry ingredients and add to pumpkin mixture. Stir until well blended. Fold in raisins and nuts. Pour into 3 or 4 greased loaf tins. Bake at 350F for one hour.

SPICED WHOLEMEAL PUMPKIN BREAD

185g butter, melted
1/2 cup honey
1 egg, lightly beaten
3 cups (375g) finely grated raw pumpkin
3/4 cup raw sugar
3 cups wholemeal self-raising flour
1 tablespoon ground cinnamon

Grease a 15cm x 25cm loaf pan, line base and sides with paper; grease paper well.

Combine butter, honey and egg in large bowl, stir in pumpkin, sugar, flour and cinnamon. Pour into prepared pan, bake in moderate oven for about 50 minutes. Stand 5 minutes before turning on to wire rack to cool. Serve with butter if desired.

BASIC PUMPKIN SCONE RECIPE

1 cup cooked pumpkin, mashed   1 tablespoon butter
1 tablespoon sugar   1 egg
2 cups self-raising flour   pinch salt

Cream butter and sugar, add mashed pumpkin. Mix in egg. Add flour gradually. Roll out and cut. Put on tray and bake for 20 minutes in oven at 400F.

PUMPKIN SCONES

28g margarine   2 cups self-raising flour
85g castor sugar   2 cups cold mashed pumpkin
1 egg, beaten   milk for glazing

Cream the margarine and sugar together. beat in the egg. Add the flour and pumpkin and mix to a soft dough. Knead lightly until smooth. Roll out until 3/4 inch thick and cut into 1-1/2 inch rounds. Place on a greased baking tray, glaze with milk and bake in a hot oven (400-450 F, 200-230 C) 15 minutes, or until cooked.

Split while warm and spread with margarine.

FRUITY PUMPKIN SCONES

2 cups wholemeal self-raising flour
2 tablespoons butter, melted
1 teaspoon ground cinnamon
2 tablespoons currants or sultanas

3/4 cooked mashed pumpkin
1 tablespoon honey
a little milk to mix

Mix pumpkin, butter, honey, cinnamon and currants or sultanas. Work in flour and add enough milk to bring to a soft dough consistency. Knead lightly and roll out and cut into 12 to 15 pieces. Bake on a greased tray at 400F or 200C for about 15 minutes. Serve hot or cold.

PUMPKIN AND POPPY SEED MUFFINS

1 cup wholemeal self-raising flour
1 cup self-raising flour
1 cup crushed weet-bix
1/4 teaspoon ground cloves
1/4 teaspoon ground cardamom
1/4 cup poppy seeds
2 teaspoons grated orange rind
1/4 cup polyunsaturated vegetable oil
3/4 cup Sanitarium So Good
1 cup mashed cooked pumpkin

Lightly grease a deep, straight-sided 12 hole muffin pan. Combine sifted self-raising flours, spices, crushed weet-bix and poppy seeds in a large bowl.

Combine rind, oil and So Good with pumpkin; mix well. Stir pumpkin mixture into dry ingredients, stir with a fork until just combined.

Spoon heaped tablespoons of mixture into prepared pan, bake in moderate oven for about 20 minutes, or until firm and golden brown. Turn muffins onto a wire rack to cool. Makes 12.

GLUTEN FREE PUMPKIN MUFFINS

1/2 cup cooked mashed pumpkin
1/2 cup melted, cooled butter
1 tablespoon baking powder
1/4 cup milk
1/4 teaspoon each of nutmeg, cinnamon and salt

2 lightly beaten eggs
1 cup rice flour, sifted
3/4 cup maize meal

Preheat oven to 175C (350F). Grease muffin tray. Mix flours, baking powder and spices. Make a well in flour mixture, add all other ingredients and mix well. Pour into tray and bake for approximately 35 minutes. Serve hot or cold, sliced and buttered.

FLO'S PUMPKIN SCONES

1 egg
1 cup cold mashed pumpkin
2-1/4 cups self-raising flour

1 tablespoon butter
1/2 cup sugar
1/4 teaspoon salt

Set oven at 225-250 degrees C. (425-450 F). Mix butter, sugar and salt in bowl. Add egg and pumpkin. Mix in flour. Turn dough onto floured board and cut into scones. Cook 15-20 minutes.

TANGY PUMPKIN SCONES

1 cup cold mashed pumpkin
2-1/2 cups self-raising flour
salt
1/2 teaspoon nutmeg
1/2 teaspoon mixed spice

2 tablespoons icing sugar
2 tablespoons butter
1 egg
1/2 cup milk
1/2 teaspoon grated lemon rind

Sift dry ingredients. Add lemon rind. Melt butter and add to egg beaten into milk. Stir liquid and pumpkin into dry mixture. Knead lightly and cut into required shapes. Cook 12-15 minutes in very hot oven.

CHEESY PUMPKIN & OAT SCONES

1 cup mashed cooked pumpkin
1 cup white self-raising flour
1/2 cup wholemeal self-raising flour
1/2 cup rolled oats

2 tablespoons margarine
1/4 teaspoon paprika
1/2 cup grated cheese
1/3 cup milk

Sift flours together into a bowl. Add oats. Rub in margarine. Add mashed pumpkin, grated cheese, milk and paprika. Mix to a soft dough.

Place scone mixture on a floured board and knead gently. Press out with palm of hand until scone mixture is about 3 cm thick. Cut with a scone cutter and place on a greased and floured scone tray. Bake at 200C (400F) for 10 to 12 minutes.

SPICY PUMPKIN SCONES

1/4 teaspoon each nutmeg and cinnamon
1/4 cup chopped walnuts
1/2 cup milk
1 egg, beaten
3/4 cup cooked mashed pumpkin

60g butter or margarine
1/4 cup castor sugar
2-1/2 cups self-raising flour
1/2 teaspoon salt

Set oven temperature at hot 220C (400F).
In a mixing bowl, cream butter and sugar until light and

53

fluffy. Stir in pumpkin and egg, mixing thoroughly. Sift flour, salt, spices and walnuts and stir into pumpkin mixture. Mix to a soft dough with milk and turn out on to a lightly floured surface. Pat or roll out to a 2 cm thickness. Stamp out rounds with a 5 cm cutter.

Place the scones on a lightly greased tray, brush with milk and bake for 15 minutes or until browned.

PUMPKIN DATE CAKE

1 tablespoon grated orange rind
250g butter
3/4 cup castor sugar
2 eggs
1 cup chopped dates
1/2 cup coconut
1/2 cup cold mashed pumpkin
2 cups self-raising flour
1/2 cup milk

Grease a deep 19cm square cake pan, line base with paper; grease paper.

Cream butter, rind and sugar in small bowl with electric mixer until light and fluffy; beat in eggs one at a time, beat until combined. Transfer mixture to large bowl, stir in dates, coconut and pumpkin. Stir in half the sifted flour and half the milk, then stir in remaining flour and milk. Spread into prepared pan. Bake in moderately slow oven for about 1-1/4 hours. Stand 5 minutes before turning on to wire rack to cool. Dust with sifted icing sugar.

ECONOMICAL PUMPKIN FRUIT CAKE

1/4 cup margarine
1 egg
1 cup mashed pumpkin
1 cup sugar
1-1/2 cups self-raising flour
3/4 packet mixed fruit

Cream butter and sugar, add egg, pumpkin and flour, lastly fruit. Bake in moderate oven.

PUMPKIN SYRUP CAKE

250g butter
2 tablespoons grated orange rind
2 tablespoons grated lemon rind
1 cup castor sugar
3 eggs, separated
2 cups self-raising flour
1 cup mashed pumpkin

Syrup
2 tablespoons orange juice
2 tablespoons lemon juice
3/4 cup sugar

Grease a deep 23cm round cake pan, line base with paper; grease paper.

Cream butter, rinds and sugar in small bowl with electric mixer until light and fluffy, add egg yolks; beat until combined. Transfer to large bowl. Stir in half the sifted flour with half the cold pumpkin, then stir in remaining flour and pumpkin.

Beat egg whites in small bowl until small peaks form, fold through cake mixture. Spread mixture into prepared pan. Bake in moderate oven for about 1 hour, pour hot syrup over hot cake. Stand 10 minutes before turning onto wire rack to cool.

Syrup:
Combine all ingredients in saucepan. Stir constantly over heat without boiling until sugar is dissolved. Bring to boil, reduce heat, simmer 2 minutes without stirring.

PUMPKIN ORANGE & SULTANA CAKE

1 cup cooked mashed pumpkin
1 dessertspoon grated orange rind
3 tablespoons butter
3/4 cup sugar
1 egg

1 cup sultanas
2 cups self-raising flour
pinch salt
1/2 cup milk

Cream butter and sugar, add egg, beating well. Add mashed pumpkin, rind, sultanas, salt and sifted flour. Stir in milk. Bake in greased cake tin about 1 hour in moderate oven.

When cold, ice with orange icing.

PUMPKIN CURRANT CAKE

2 cups cooked mashed pumpkin
3/4 cup honey
1 tablespoon mixed spice
2-1/2 cups wholemeal self-raising flour

1/2 cup melted butter
2 cups currants

Mix pumpkin, honey, spice, butter and currants well, and stir in the flour, mixing thoroughly. Place in greased baking tin and bake at 350F or 180C for 40 to 45 minutes. Serve hot or cold.

PUMPKIN CAKE

1 dessertspoon golden syrup
1 cup cooked, mashed pumpkin
2 cups mixed fruit
1/4 teaspoon nutmeg/cinnamon (optional)

2 eggs
2 cups self-raising flour
1/2 cup butter
1 cup sugar

Cream butter and sugar, golden syrup and pumpkin. Add eggs one at a time, then flour and fruit. Bake in a 21cm round or square tin for 1-1/2 hours in a moderate oven. Nice spread with butter.

PUMPKIN JAFFA CAKE

125g butter
2 teaspoons grated orange rind
1/2 cup castor sugar
1 egg
1 tablespoon golden syrup
3/4 cup cold mashed pumpkin
1-1/4 cups self-raising flour
1/2 teaspoon bicarbonate of soda
2 tablespoons cocoa
1 tablespoon custard powder
1/4 cup orange juice

Chocolate Icing
1 cup icing sugar
1 tablespoon cocoa
1 teaspoon butter
1 tablespoon milk

Grease a 14cm x 21cm loaf pan, line base with paper; grease paper.

Cream butter, rind and sugar in small bowl with electric mixer only until combined. Beat in egg and golden syrup, transfer to large bowl. Stir in pumpkin, then half the sifted dry ingredients and orange juice. Pour mixture into prepared pan. Bake in moderate oven for about 1 hour, stand 5 minutes before turning onto wire rack to cool. Spread cold cake with icing.

Chocolate Icing:
Sift icing sugar and cocoa into small heatproof bowl, stir in butter and enough milk to make a stiff paste. Stir over hot water until icing is spreadable.

PUMPKIN CAKE WITH FRUIT AND NUTS

2 teaspoons mixed spice
2 cups cooked mashed pumpkin
4 eggs, well beaten
2 teaspoons vanilla
1 cup chopped nuts
1 cup raisins or other dried fruit

1-1/2 cups butter or corn oil
2 cups sugar
3-1/2 cups flour
2 teaspoons baking powder
2 teaspoons bicarb soda
1 teaspoon salt

Cream together butter and sugar. Sift together dry ingredients, using 1 cup of the flour and add to creamed mixture along with the pumpkin. Add eggs and vanilla, beating well. Fold in nuts and raisins, which have been mixed with remaining 1/2 cup flour. Bake in a greased and floured loaf pan in a moderately hot oven for 60 minutes.

PUMPKIN FRUIT CAKE

1 cup cooked mashed pumpkin
2 cups self-raising flour
2 teaspoons mixed spice
2 cups mixed fruit

1 cup brown sugar
125g butter, softened
2 eggs

Cream the butter and sugar. Beat in the eggs one at a time, combining well, then add the cold mashed pumpkin. Sift together the flour and mixed spice; add the mixed fruit. Pour the mixture into a greased 20cm cake tin and bake in a moderately slow oven for one hour, or until cooked when tested. Cool the cake on a wire rack. If possible the cake is best stored for two to three days before cutting.

GLUTEN FREE PUMPKIN CAKE

1/2 cup softened butter
1 cup grated peeled pumpkin
1/2 cup raw sugar
1 tablespoon honey
1-1/4 cups millet flour

2 eggs
2 teaspoons cinnamon
1/2 teaspoon bicarbonate of soda
pinch salt
1/2 cup chopped pumpkin seeds

Preheat oven to 160C (325F). Grease a 20cm cake tin, or small loaf tin. Cream sugar and butter in large bowl, add eggs and mix. Add all other ingredients and mix well. Pour into cake tin and bake approximately 50 minutes. When cold, cake could be iced and decorated with chopped pumpkin seeds.

PUMPKIN CAKE WITH PRUNES

1 cup castor sugar
1 teaspoon grated orange rind
3 eggs
1/4 cup orange juice
3/4 cup cold mashed pumpkin (not butternut pumpkin)

250g butter
1/2 cup finely chopped prunes
2 cups self-raising flour
1/3 cup milk, approximately

Cream butter, orange rind and sugar together until light and fluffy, add eggs one at a time, beating well after each addition. Stir in orange juice, pumpkin and prunes, then sifted flour alternately with enough milk to give a soft consistency. Spread into greased deep 20cm round cake tin with base lined with greaseproof paper, bake in moderate oven 1 to 1-1/4 hours, stand 5 minutes, turn onto wire rack to cool.

59

BARBARA'S PUMPKIN CITRUS CHEESECAKE

Crust
250g plain sweet biscuits
170g butter
Filling
250g packaged cream cheese   1 teaspoon grated lemon rind
3/4 cup castor sugar   1 teaspoon grated orange rind
2 eggs, separated   1 tablespoon lemon juice
1 tablespoon gelatine   1 tablespoon orange juice
1 teaspoon icing sugar   1-1/2 cups cream
2 tablespoons water   1/4 cup sugar extra
1 cup cold cooked mashed pumpkin pushed through sieve

Crust
    Combine finely crushed biscuit crumbs with melted butter; mix well. Press over sides and base of greased 21cm springform pan.

Filling
    Sprinkle gelatine over water, dissolve over hot water. Beat cream cheese and sugar until smooth. Beat egg yolks and extra sugar with spoon in top of double saucepan until light and creamy. Put over simmering water; stir until sugar dissolves and mixture is thick. Remove from heat; add dissolved gelatine. Gradually add egg yolk mixture to cream cheese mixture; beat until smooth.
    Fold pumpkin into cream cheese mixture with lemon and orange juice and rind. Whip cream, fold half into pumpkin mixture. Lastly fold in beaten egg whites, spoon into crumb crust, refrigerate until set.
    Fold grated orange and lemon rind into remaining whipped cream with 1 teaspoon icing sugar. Spread over top of cheesecake.

WHOLEMEAL PUMPKIN AND FIG CAKE

1-1/2 cups strong black tea
90g butter
2/3 cup sultanas
1 cup chopped dried figs
2 teaspoons grated lemon rind
1-1/4 cups wholemeal plain flour
1/2 cup wholemeal self-raising flour
1/2 teaspoon bicarbonate of soda

1/2 teaspoon ground nutmeg
1/2 teaspoon ground cinnamon
1/2 teaspoon ground ginger
3/4 cup cold mashed pumpkin

Lightly grease a 14cm x 21cm loaf pan, cover base with greased paper. Place tea, butter, sultanas, figs and lemon rind in a medium saucepan, stir over heat until butter is melted. Bring to the boil, reduce heat, cover and simmer for ten minutes. Remove from heat and remove mixture to a large bowl; leave to cool to room temperature.

Sift flours, soda and spices over fruit mixture in bowl; mix well. Add pumpkin to fruit mixture and mix well. Spread mixture into prepared pan, bake in moderate oven for about 1 hour, or until cooked when tested. Cover with foil and leave to cool in pan.

Growing and Caring for Pumpkins

From the Organic Gardening Seasonal Guide and Calendar
published annually in September.
($9.00 post paid from Southern Holdings, P.O. Huonville 7109)

Pumpkins are all members of the cucurbit family. They
are vines, and are all killed by frost. They need lots of warm
weather to produce. Pumpkins are gross feeders, so the
more compost in the soil the better; they also need lots of
room to grow. The small-scale gardener sometimes trains
them against a fence, putting the larger fruits into slings to
support them while growing. The gardener with lots of space
will put a rock or tin can under the maturing fruit, to prevent
rotting of the part that would otherwise be in contact with
the ground. The members of this family are all very competi-
tive with weeds and are fast growing, so little in the way of
weeding is needed after the first few weeks.

Since they like heat, it is a good idea in cooler areas to
delay mulching until the ground has thoroughly warmed up.
Some growers overcome this by using large rocks as a
mulch. The rocks absorb heat during the day and release it
at night, ameliorating the climate around the plants.

The cucurbits rely on insect pollination to set fruit. When
these are in short supply, the gardener has to step in. The
female flower has a swelling at the base which is the imma-
ture fruit. The male flower has no swelling. A male flower is
stripped of its petals and the protuberance bearing the pol-
len brushed against the female counterpart. One male flower
is good for four or five females. The flowers must be abso-
lutely fresh. By hand pollinating, nearly every female flower
will set fruit. The growing tips of the vines can be pinched off
when any further fruits that set are unlikely to ripen. The end

of the main leader will produce more side branches, which are more fruitful, when pinched off at a length of about one metre.

Like tomatoes, cucurbits hate wet leaves. Water in the morning and under the leaf canopy if at all possible. Water regularly and deeply, yield is severely restricted when water supply is uneven.

There is an amazing variety of pumpkins, both in appearance and in flavour. There are actually two sorts, winter squash and true pumpkins, but there is no cultural difference as far as the gardener is concerned. Their main characteristic is the setting of sweet fruit that has a hard skin, many of them keeping very well because of it. The size of the fruit varies from the size of a grapefruit in the case of the bush variety 'Golden Nugget' to the 50 kg of the large vined 'Big Max'. In between there are a multitude of colours, shapes and sizes, pink, red, yellow, green, banana, spherical, ribbed, acorn and turban. Try a sowing of each until you know the sorts you like and which do well in your district. Some have moist flesh, some dry and some more or less sweet. The keeping quality appeals in some and the exquisite flavour in others. One of our favourites is 'Green Warty Hubbard', a winter squash. The skin is so tough it has to be broken into with an axe! It keeps well though, we like the taste and the famous keeper, 'Queensland Blue', does not ripen in our cool climate (Tasmania).

Pumpkins are best picked fully mature. For storage, they should be ripened in the sun, turning regularly to expose all sides. If a frost seems likely, cover them or carry them indoors overnight. Well ripened pumpkins of some varieties will keep for two years or more. Make sure you leave the stalk on though. Do not use it for a carrying handle. Damage at the junction of the stalk and fruit allows rots in. Store them in an airy, dry place, spaced away from each other to prevent rots spreading.

Pumpkin Varieties   Comments

Bush types

Bush Table Queen	Sweet, dry flesh. Good for baking whole.
Golden Nugget	Grapefruit size. Good keeper.
Butterbush	Butternut type and flavour.

Medium Vines

Baby Blue	Small fruit, very dry, very sweet. Good keeper.
Buttercup.	Dry flesh.
Hercules Butternut	Large butternut. Keeps well. Stands adverse weather.

Large Vines

Big Max	Good for largest pumpkin competitions.
Blue Banana	Fruit up to 1 metre in length, tasty.
Crown Prince	Excellent keeper.
Golden Delicious	Fast maturing, very tasty, poor keeper.
Henderson Late Grey	Good keeper.
Jarrahdale	Good keeper.
Queensland Blue	Good keeper.
Red Hubbard	Large, firm flesh.
Green Warted Hubbard	Large, tasty, tough skin, good keeper.
Triamble	Good keeper.
Windsor Black	Early maturing.
Tripletreat	Hull-less seeds, good keeper.

Giant Pumpkins - A Way of Life

The GIANT PUMPKIN growing craze began in 1893 at the St Louis USA World Fair, where a 165kg pumpkin set a world record that lasted 73 years. The current record was set in 1993 with a 380kg pumpkin (it's in the Guiness Book of Records).

The World Pumpkin Confederation (WPC) holds annual pumpkin weigh-offs throughout the World, including Australian sites in VIC, WA, NSW & ACT. The current Aus. Record is held by Steven Jeffery of Coffs Harbour (228kg in 1993). Detailed information is available from the WPC Southern Hemisphere Office: *C/- Karingal Hub Shopping Centre, 330 Cranbourne Rd, Frankston, 3199.*

ATLANTIC GIANT Pumpkins are very easy to grow, taking 5 months from planting a seed to the giant harvest. They need regular feeding, watering, care and the occasional chat. Full information about growing giant vegetables, seeds and a mail order catalogue are available from Wendy and George Stayner *at Atlantic Seeds, PO Box 205, Seaford 3198, or Phone/Fax: (03)7860337.*

Best-selling Recipe Books
from Southern Holdings Pty. Ltd.

The Australian Apple Recipe Book
Includes 148 top recipes, plus orchard photographs and calendar, apple varieties, and historical apples. 10th reprint.

The Australian Banana Recipe Book
Straight from tropical Queensland comes this extensive range of fabulous banana recipes – now this universal health food can be fully explored. Includes banana details and pictures.

The Australian Convict Recipe Book
Includes 150 practical recipes plus historical photographs, convict rules and rations and the unabridged story of Bessie Baldwin.

The Australian Historical Recipe Book
Join John Caire in exploring Australia's most popular recipes over the years, including some introduced from Europe and Asia. Includes historical photographs and the story 'Living Off The Land'. Features Bush & Spade recipes, Steamboat cooking, and Homestead recipes, as well as John's own restaurant recipes.

The Australian Huon Valley Recipe Book
Authentic country recipes from the fine food centre of Tasmania. Selected from treasured family recipe collections. Beautiful Huon scenes and the settlement story are included.

The Australian National Trust Recipe Book
A balanced collection of the most popular tried and true family recipes; this is a book to treasure over the years to come.

The Australian Potato Surprise Recipe Book
155 top Potato recipes for all occasions: the versatility of this universal food is fully exploited - a must for every kitchen.

The Great Australian Bite Recipe Book
An exciting approach to Barbecues by a top chef. Marinades, butters, breads, kebabs and barbecues galore combine to make this a 'must have' recipe book!

The Great Australian Pumpkin Recipe Book
Includes 110 pumpkin recipes (including ice cream), plus the Great Pumpkin story and Growing & Caring for Pumpkins.

Recipe Books per copy: $7.95 (GST Inc.) plus $3.30 postage and packing
(Fundraisers, please enquire about our special offer)
ORDER by MAIL, PHONE, FAX or E-MAIL from
Southern Holdings Pty Ltd P.O. Box 449, Rosny Park 7018
Phone: (03) 6247 7405 Fax: (03) 6247 1116
E-Mail bookagencies@trump.net.au